The Middle of the Journey

Alabama Poetry Series

General Editors: Dara Wier and Thomas Rabbitt

The Middle
of the Journey

BRIAN SWANN

The University of Alabama Press

Publication of this book has been assisted
by a grant from the
Andrew W. Mellon Foundation.

Library of Congress Cataloging in Publication Data

Swann, Brian.
  The Middle of the Journey.

  (The Alabama poetry series)
  I. Title.   II. Series.
PS3569.W256M5   811'.54   81-14831
ISBN 0-8173-0084-8   AACR2
ISBN 0-8173-0095-3 (pbk.)

The artwork on the title page is
by Nahum Tschacbasov. Used by permission.

The last four lines of "Legend" are adapted from a War (or Wolf) Song sung
by Gray Hawk. See *Teton Sioux Music* by Frances Densmore (Smithsonian
Institution, Bureau of American Ethnology, Bulletin 61, 1918).

This book is dedicated

to the memory of my father,

Stanley F. Swann,

(born Cambridge, England, May 13, 1909;

died Cambridge, England, May 16, 1978).

Other Books by Brian Swann

Poetry:

The Whale's Scars (1975).
Roots (1976).
Living Time (1978).
The Four Seasons (1981).

Fiction:

The Runner (1980).
Elizabeth (1981).
Unreal Estate (1981).

Children:

The Fox and the Buffalo (1982).

Translation:

The Collected Poems of Lucio Piccolo, translated and edited with Ruth Feldman, (1972).
Shema: Collected Poems of Primo Levi, with Feldman, (1975).
Selected Poetry of Andrea Zanzotto, translated with Feldman, (1976).
The Day is Always New: Selected Poems of Rocco Scotellaro, with Feldman, (1981).
The Dry Air of the Fire: Selected Poems of Bartolo Cattafi, with Feldman, (1981).
The Moon of the Bourbons: Selected Poems of Vittorio Bodini, with Feldman, (1981).
Primele Poeme/First Poems of Tristan Tzara, with Michael Impey, (1975).
Selected Poems of Tudor Arghezi, with Impey, (1976).
Euripides' Phoenissae, translated with Peter Burian, (1981).
On the Nomad Sea: Selected Poems of Milih Cevdet Anday, with Talat Halman, (1981).
Song of the Sky: Versions of Native American Poetry, (1982).

Editing:

Currents and Trends: Italian Poetry Today, with Feldman, (1979).
Smoothing The Ground: Essays on Native American Oral Literature, (1982).

Contents

Acknowledgments

I would like to thank the National Endowment for the Arts for a Fellowship, and CAPS (Creative Artists in the Public Service) for a grant.

Some of the poems in this collection have appeared in the following journals, sometimes in earlier versions with different titles. Grateful acknowledgment is made to the following:

The American Scholar: "Red Umbrella" (Autumn 1979). Copyright ©1979 by Brian Swann.

The Antioch Review: "Driving Off." Copyright © 1979 by The Antioch Review, Inc. First published in *The Antioch Review*, Vol. 37, No. 3 (Summer 1979). Reprinted by permission of the editors.

The Beloit Poetry Journal: "Potlatch." First published in *The Beloit Poetry Journal*, Vol. 29, No. 4 (Summer 1979).

Black Warrior Review: "Face." Originally published as "Light" in Vol. 7, No. 1 (Fall 1980).

Bennington Review: "The Middle of the Journey" (Winter 1982).

Canto: "Turtle Fountain." Originally published in *Canto*, Vol. 3, No. 1 (1979).

The Carleton Miscellany: "The Conquest of Wandlebury" in Vol. 18, No. 1 (Winter 1979).

Chouteau Review: "The Women" in Vol. 5, No. 1 (Fall 1981).

Cincinnati Poetry Review: "Skirt." First published in *Cincinnati Poetry Review*, No. 6 (Fall 1979).

Harper's: "Joy" (in press).

Invisible City: "Backlog" in Vol. 26–27 (August 1980).

Kayak: "Moon of Ripening Berries" in Vol. 55 (January 1981); "Following Through" in Vol. 56 (July 1981).

The Literary Review: "Nexus." Reprinted from *The Literary Review*, Vol. 24, No. 3 (Spring 1981), published by Fairleigh Dickinson University.

The Massachusetts Review: "The Soul in Parenthesis" in Vol. 22, No. 2 (Summer 1981).

Mid-American Review: "Late Spring" in Vol. 1, No. 1 (Spring 1981).

Mississippi Review: "Cousin Annie" in Vol. 8, No. 3 (Fall 1979).

The Nation: "Legend." First published in *The Nation* (January 1978).

The New Yorker: "Back." Copyright © 1979, The New Yorker Magazine, Inc.; "Like Boats." Copyright © 1981, The New Yorker Magazine, Inc.

The New York Arts Journal: "Leaving." First published in *New York Arts Journal*, issue 2.

Partisan Review: "Fairy Tale." First published in *Partisan Review*, Vol. XLV, No. 3 (1978).

The Pawn Review: "A Bird Passes" in Vol. 3, No. 1, No. 2 (1978–1979).

Pequod: "Zero at the Bone" in Vol. 2, No. 4 (1978).

Poetry: "Unknowing" (December 1972).

Salmagundi: "Nights" (Winter 1982).

San José Studies: "Indian Summer," "The Truth" in Vol. 6, No. 1 (February 1980).

ONE

(i)
Reflections

Red Umbrella

You go along. Your father dies. You
walk into the kitchen one morning. It
is bright. Your father is there. Your
mother is there. You smile at your
mother. Your mother is radiance. You
wake with your face and pillow wet.
Your hands hurt with climbing a fence
to the roof. From there you can see
all along the gardens. Fruit trees,
asparagus on raised beds. Birds
fly up to you. The fence high as
a house bends. You are on your
hands and knees grubbing in the soil.
You go along. Your father is dead.
Someone who shares a shelter
from the rain with you says:
I was once in the China Sea.
There was a typhoon. The rain
came in silver sheets. Each wave
brought its own curtain of rain.
The boats were dragging their
anchors. We were all on deck in
life jackets. I was young so I
had no thoughts of death. You
say, it'll let up in ten minutes.
Water slicked with oil
runs in gutters like rope. He
jumps into the storm, sticking
a red umbrella out at it.
The sun gives a gray glow. You
watch the birds. You
go along.

Face

When I arrived after
the moon had just set,
cherry blossoms still made
a white night, the moon
still in it, drifting
over and around me.
The lilac hid its scent
in the hawthorn.
A note in a strange hand said
Don't go in. A light shone
in his bedroom window.

*

The pond he and I'd dug
hugs its last year leaves.
The child totters and
almost falls
into their slime.

The grass, even the
new sown, is silver
with seed. The new fence
is not yet part
of my world.
The elm with an arm sawn off
is almost another tree.
The fence is higher
than the one blown over
in a succession of small winds.

In the window of his room's
door-length balcony
a face.
It doesn't seem to see
what's there.
Its roses are late.

Nights

The face is gray clay. The nose
a handle to hold it by, bigger
than life, its roots sunk
into cavities slowly
growing larger. The terrible
gray eyes of my childhood are
clamped shut. But still there.
A little crumb of dried
snot inside the nostril.
A lump under the white sheet
must be his hands but
could be embalmed viscera.
There is a chemical coldness
about the brow. This is his
last bed. But down the hall
my mother still sees him
carrying buckets of rainwater
from the yard to their bedroom,
tipping them gently over
the plants on the miniature
balcony he built jutting
over the garden. Cyclamen,
fuchsia, and small lighted
buttons squander themselves
in colors unreal as a
hummingbird's breast that
is no color, all reflection.
Those first nights sleep
was not easy. Sounds
came to the cave mouth.
Night did not just
come and go. It tugged
this way and that.

Second Hand

The 23rd Psalm came
and went while I slowly
spelled out the names
pro patria mori.
A Sergeant Mitra seemed out
of place, but his polished brass
still gilded the mouths of lilies.
It was hard to imagine
fire behind them.
                    My sister
would not forgive the cremation.
But it was his wish.
Burial refused
to release you
to stars.
          "There are millions of
universes out there," he said, walking me
out into the cold night
day hid. "There's life."
                    I should
have said: "There are millions
of universes here, too."
                    "We are
so insignificant," he told the sky.

I slipped back into the house.
A shiver caught me.
I sat down and counted the commonplace
dishes kept for best and never used.
I watched the clock pile up time,
then lose it with the sweep
of its second hand.

Reflections

My grandmother and aunt took off
his oil-soaked clothes and
bathed him like a baby.
He didn't know where he was.
The Navy took him to King's Seat.
My mother said: "Tall lovely Americans
sat playing with their fingers
in corridor after corridor."
Light drifted through high windows.
All you could hear was the
thin sound of breathing.
He sat in the corner, alone,
on a bench. He leaped away
from her. "I don't know you,"
he said. His mind has stopped,
the doctor whispered. Bring
the baby with you next time.
"You brought him round. We still
don't know what he's been through
all those years. You have to
make allowances. Have to."

The nose and its small broken veins
is whiter than my mother's powder
he used on it before venturing out.
It is sealed, the gray eye
with its cinder trapped
like an insect. In his rages
it was my awful focus.
My sister weeps. "Goodbye daddy.
I haven't called you that
in a long time." She wants to
kiss him, but is afraid. She
touches him instead. "He only said,
'Be kind, be nice.' "
                        Cold summer
air from the open window
above the casket thrums like wind
through the rigging of a ship.

7

The death-mask is calm
after the explosion in the heart
that took him off where
depth-charge and torpedo
could not.

       The morning I leave,
fen cirrus feathers over the sun.
A heron's curved prow sails over
the railroad sidings.
There's a reflection in the coach window.
The reflections go on as we pick up
speed. The reflections
go with us.

His Voice

Each waking's a forgetting. I
close my eyes again.

Far off, as if it had not
happened yet, I see my father

Pull close the curtains on
the still-light street. I hear

His voice: "Let's close out the world,"
it says, seductive, authoritative, dead.

Legacy

Him,
hiding in folds of earth,
lost in sounds of dark
green, refusing to come out
except on nights when plants
glow with old stored light
and the cold sky creaks
like an old door
and stars
shoot out of place as if
they knew where they were going,
and his mind, slowly moving
into mine
when it finally
gave out.

Polaris

The moon's yellow plain slopes away.
My father points out the north star to my mother
who has been looking for it in the opposite direction.
There are no trees to impede the star;
no lakes, no clouds, no rivers, no towns.
The silence is the silence of steel,
or as if an invisible music
is waiting to make everything
alright, touch the scene with more
than is actually there,
more than a scene on the bare moon,
my mother looking one way, perhaps
for Polaris, my father certainly looking
for it, and finding it,
the only star in the night sky,
though he too perhaps is only
pretending to look, really wishing
to turn round away from his knowledge
and look behind at the immense
blackness my mother is watching.

Mother and Father

With one breath the
    river's out.
                    Mother
leaves my side and
    crosses the room.
Granite leans through
    the window. She is
following the calls of
    the Master of Throws
who tosses at my feet
    unmarked dice, coffin-
shaped. I pry them
    open. Nothing. Eat,
says my mother, handing
    me an egg. The sky
stiffens as she crosses
    away from me, the
candlelit waters of her
    bridal gown blow blue
with one breath, then
    flow as the river
at night.
                    The river
curves ahead like a
    sickle. Bridges strain
from each bank. Father
    is a face in the
undertow. His hand takes
    the drowned light
from her gown and
    moves it ahead
like dark.

Turtle Fountain

Light is sidetracked by open
french windows; swarms in

like bees swerving from
danced directions. Grandmother,

mother, aunt, sister, sit
in a row. I turn my grandmother's

face sideways against the light's
scattered pollen. My sister

sobs. I try to recall if
I'd told them the truth:

my father, old trickster,
he who had beaten his backside

black and blue for not keeping
guard while he slept, is

not dead. He has covered his
tracks, right down to the

plastic manikin he left in
his casket. "It's not him,"

my mother had said. She didn't know
how right she was. But I knew

the city he'd left for. I'd have
no trouble finding the small piazza

he'd chosen to live in. The one
with a fountain; four small boys

pushing turtles over the rim
back under the main fall of water.

(ii)
Back

A Visit to the Old Country

The child on my knee pretends to read,
pointing to the place with conviction
in what she calls her 'bone book'.

She knows that beneath the skin are bones,
and rattles them off as I touch her:
What's under here? I ask.
Radius, ulna, tibia, fibula, scapula—
she knows them all, but,
impatient to be on with the real business,
she gets another book, and 'reads':

Eggs in the pot,
eggs in the pot,
eggs split in the pot,
O! O! O!

Bite the fish, dame.
Bite the fish, dame.
Bite the fish, black one.
Bite the fish black.
O! O! O!

*

The encyclopedia falls off the edge of the chair,
lying face up at a man chased by a bull.

*

Leaves go up,
leaves go down,
leaves go shelter
in the cave.

*

I had walked round the town of my adolescence.
Nothing was the same, and
everything was the same.

*

Once upon a time there were lots of prehistoric animals.
I will tell you it tomorrow.
Go away to bed.

*

I hold the child light as a leaf.
I teach her to eat dry fruit and tell her about seeds
that go through her and become trees.

*

My father has taken down a tree and heightened a fence.
He and I sit up all night talking.
I can tell him nothing.

*

The house is raw damp though he has
put in his own central heating.
My feet never thaw.
There is no ice on the fishpond.
There are no fish.

*

He worships the child on his knee.
She trusts him completely.

*

She asks me to be a monster or a ghost.
A screech and howl and she runs screaming.

*

I am tired.
I sleep twelve hours.
She wakes me at noon,
kisses me, asks me to be a ghost.
I say I have already, but she wants more.
And I rise wailing.

*

She follows me everywhere.
When I have dressed I ask her for more stories.
Under condensing windows she tells me:

> Once upon a time there was some celery and a tomato. Their
> pan was in a brick house and the parents didn't like taking their
> children to school. The mother was a tomato and the father
> celery. One day their children vanished and the mother and the
> father ate two carrots, two tomatoes, one pea, one potato, and
> an onion. And then they went to see where their children had
> gone, but they couldn't find them. They never found them. The
> end.

Moon of Ripening Berries

A black back rises and turns
over. You are born. Glory
to the leaves that have brought you
thus far.
       Last night the water
was high. The moon flared and
sank. Where the wind is now
was just dry leaves.
             Something
has fallen off the raft.
A spider suspends her nest
over the water, full of granular
replicas. You are born. Nets
sway for something to catch
onto. Unrest enters the world
that will not make way.
Silence already trapped is
flowing away. Your feet are
wrapped in yesterday's newspaper.
Your skin is verdigris
and loose; it does not fit.
A ventriloquist's light
shines through you. A fish cuts
across, and then is fish
again.
      Into high collapsing
summer you are born. The moon
is gravid, and stammers. It is
full of water. Your hand is
already disfigured by the clasped
stone. Already you are walking.
The desert stands revealed
at noon. Take your cup to
the center. Wait. Soon
moon shallows will return
reflections. The mirror has no
back. You are born.

Bloodroot
flowers have closed, clear as water.
The single leaf folds round.
As sap shrinks into the swollen
root, air tastes the damp night
smoke of old logs. At the tip
of a saxifrage root you are
born.

On the hand measuring
spans to the zenith a solitary
butterfly settles. He has swallowed
most of the sky. He will not burn.
He flies on the tide.
He is the heart of devastated
soil. He is the shadow
of exhausted air. As he opens
his mouth for moisture
you are born.

Something
drops onto your hair. You are the soft
hiatus before fall. You are
sinking back toward twilight
with your face full of the sun.
You are fragrant. Beggarticks
and sticktights snatch at you,
till the loon's ghost-call
shivers off the lake. Your tears
stud Orion's belt. Cygnus
shakes in the eastern sky.
In the locked room, something
is beginning to smell like snow.
You are born.

Starlight
is in the boat. Eight young women
hang their clothes on the lower
branches of spruce and slip
into the lake. Ripples inter-

lock and lock them in.
They move in wide arcs away.
Green mirrors open
in the woods. A splash peels
back the dark. The lodestar
loses itself in its reflection,
and fades. Something passing
is known by the slow straightening
of grass, leaves brushed free
of dew.
        You are born.
              There is
blood still in your eyes. The sky
is getting bigger by the hour. The boat
stretches its rope. Minims of waves
clatter up the rockface. The boat
pivots like a compass needle.
The sun has cold in it, pushing through.
You are born.
        The flies have found you.

Back

This light is more than the light
that gets into the wind and makes it

depths and warm places, great pits
where the light comes and goes,

freeing itself from the river that
runs between charred prairie flowers

and wild vines when autumn fires have
swept the land black, and the only green

grows dully on islands. This light is
a child I wonder if I'll meet again

before it is too late. A child
who walks among skies of enormous blue

engined by the bursts of great stars.
He has taken a number of different

names. In his early world I wonder
if I'll find him sad, or smiling

inside a glass dome that settles over
everything as the sun fuses itself

into a quartz crystal, and birds,
as if carved from the branches they

perch on, retrace the same songs
again and again, each time somehow

different. There is a mirror the child
has hung in the woods. I would like

to walk toward it, right through
the depth, and keep going

forward, going, in fact, back.

Late Spring

Through the window I watch
the shadblow fall into
cold fragments. Petals of

White form a sky and confuse
the glass. Through a spider's
close chambers an invisible

Clue of wind ripples, darkening
the silk, leaving it light. I stand.
I cross the pasture. By

The pilings in the boatyard
fish turn with some
urgency. I watch one

Rise to a petal. I try
tracing things back to
real things. And turn

Round to where the house
seems to enclose its own shell,
and all the rooms echo

Each other. I hear my mother's
voice calling me by name.
It doesn't seem my name.

It doesn't seem like anybody's
name. The night before I had
dreamed of swimming. A hand

From below grasped my ankle
with small gentle fingers. Now,
from behind the house I can smell

Smoke from the rakings, giving out.
Scents of light rain. On the
top of the maple hanging few leaves

I can see the wing of a bird
brightening. The fire flares.
A shoulder of smoke collects

The storm gray and floats it off.
Everything is dissolved into
the derangement of late spring.

This morning I dug out
the streambed. A newt, commonest
of salamanders, startling

In adolescent pink, reached for
a rotten leaf with perfect fingers
of its left hand, missed, and

Corrected. Its eyes of damp soot
ducked under a stone, as new water
gathered over its head. It leaned

Against the fresh fall of water.
Rain is threatening again. I walk
back to the house, through the shadblow's

Confusion of seasons. I sit in my old seat,
while the window fills and clears.
Gray empty halls of the spider billow

And sag like old filmy lungs. The
small perfect hands had taken
my ankle. I swam for the shore, bent

Down, and pulled out a boy, white
as a frog belly, three years on
the bottom.

Wind filters through the web
stirring trains of images. The spider
from a far corner tugs on one

Of the brittle skeins, holds it for
a moment, then lets it fall.
The thread slackens, drops,

And drifts. Soon, along the wood's
damp places, newts in adult
lighted green will high-step through

Rotting leaves and fresh shoots.
They will head for rivers and
streams where they'll hang

As if suspended from a thread.

Tracing

Green faces have parted the ferns.
    The sumac trembles. All night,
while the gale bats stars about
    like ducks, the boy's heart
kicks in its bed. Till the faces
    call to it; stride it like a spear
from beneath three blankets
    over quartz and granite
over stumps smouldering with decay
    to a burnt-out clearing by the cliff,
where it watches a child
    try to trace the star-shadow
of his head declining
    over the blue rock,
moving closer and closer to the edge.

Other Natures

Chewed-over acres. Quarry dross
falling like dunes into woods.

Shale rising in sun & wind.
The leaf turned over loses itself.

The soil's scraped from this path.
Takes on other natures, each lost

in the other, my two minds.

The wind is sucking out
the wood's light.

I have aged.

(iii)
Home Movies

The Women

in my life
smelled of lilies-of-the-valley
and picked all the flowers
they could see or smell
except hawthorn
which was unlucky.

*

Superstition never spoke
the word spelled
'p-i-g'.
For reasons of decorum
the women never said
shit, only
s-h-i-t.
But once my mother said
"Shit, the war's
over!"

*

The women believed
thunder was
Auld Nick
clomping around the upper air
in his pitman's clogs.
In storms
they turned off all the lights.
They covered my head with their aprons.

*

The women in my life
knew all the copulation
ever done by night or day
in ditches, stables, beds, huts,
byres, dank tool sheds,
in fields, on fertile allotments.
Their hands seldom let me alone.

*

At the moment of
New Year,
first-footers, the first
dark men to cross
the threshold, faces
smudgy with cork, and with coal
in their pockets,
used custom as excuse
for free kisses.
Once my aunt knocked
my mother off
a stool.
My grandmother went for
her rolling-pin.
My mother screamed.
I yelled, beating
with my fists
first one
and then the other.
The years came in
on warm feet.

*

While their men dug coal,
dealt in the black market,
made ships, sailed or repaired them,
the women were my flotilla.
They launched themselves
against my enemies
or kids who soon
became my enemies.

*

All my women
kept their word.
They promised to return
and haunt me.

29

Skirt

You follow the lady with white
light for skirts. Little mirrors

screen her from you, and hurt
your eyes. As you walk, you

practise bending from the hips
to stop your cuffs from

wearing away against the grit.
Your schoolfellows have

large noses and twisted backs.
You are tired, and your eyes

hurt. At night you bury your
eyes in her skirt so they

light up. Sometimes they catch
the tail-end of the phantom

in all its sadness. Sometimes
it is hideous with saucer

eyes, and whispers about
the boot in the groin.

And sometimes the skirt is
so far off it cannot cover the

black light that begins to
come off the sea, nor

explain the antlers drifting
in the moon's full tide.

Nexus

Jeder Engel ist schreklich

One of their subjects had seen an Angel
under similar circumstances. But this time

they reported that all they saw was violet
fluorspar on a fire of glowing coals,

and then, when they returned, an after-
image of a yellow spot on a darker ground,

looking like the sun in a deep pool.
Later, it seemed to them as if a human

figure had lengthened and begun holding
a baby; a figure with black hair, in

black sweater, black slacks, poised
at the top of basement steps, going

down. When last seen, the girl was
in the basement with the Angel's

head on her lap. In the woods
a blanket was spread, and an untouched picnic.

Aunt Gemma

Autumn filters through the glass cases
and clings to the ceiling like a web.

Her head is poised beside a golden
Don Luis and a pale Grappa. Her body's

a tinted glass figurine. Stiff
flounders and sea-bream are posed on

stained ice. Her fingers rest on the
hilt of a short knife. A gust

from the sun sharpens her hair
and twitches her red skirt.

Her face is searching the street
with its broken bottles and

graffiti: merda, puttana, boia. It
is too late. Everything is glass.

Cousin Annie

To start a kettle of beans boiling, she'd throw
a tennis ball at it. The gunk would lift the lid
and flow all over the floor. "It's a chemistry experiment,"
she'd say. "One we did in school years ago."
And she'd scoot, at the mention of school,
to what she called her thesaurus, to discover
she claimed, an article on gulls,
"with all the derivations." She'd flip,
retrace, then settle with a chewed finger
on the spot. "I always thought they were just
gulls. But it says here there are
hundreds of different kinds. This one, *this* one,
for instance, flying against the Tower of London,
is known by the fluttering of the feathers
at the tips of its wings. They bend and give,
so the bird isn't knocked about in a strong gale.
There, off he goes with the wind, unhurt. *There*."
She'd nod her head. "And here,
at the bottom. You know why gulls soar?
It's to fool the fish. Look, it says here
fish would be spooked by anything above them
moving fast, like a swallow or a bat.
The gulls know this. So they soar.
When they're ready—pow! Down they come
like a dart." She'd leave the book and rush
to polish some airy pan. She'd shiver.
"I'm cold. I'm always cold. Feel my feet."
"You're hardly wearing anything," I'd say.
"It's not that kind of cold. I'm *cold*."
And off she'd go to warm her cold nightie
by putting it carefully under her cold blanket.

Uncle Jack

His mother even
called him 'The Mark'.
Only moved when he had to—
like when cops chased him
over a cliff.
         Hid me in drawers
among linen, but when air-raid sirens
yowled he'd grab me & skip
for the shelter, pillowcases or
petticoats trailing, spirits
on his matinee-idol moustache,
shrapnel thumping into flowerbeds
from a day puffy with smoke.

Down under blossoms
his songs pushed at the roots,
and I touched the black-market
scar that shaped his face,
the blue & glass
folded in.

The Conquest of Wandlebury

A child who knew her age but not
what struck or buried her under
the lips of the inner ramparts.
A young woman they couldn't age more accurately
than under twenty, her legs missing,
buried before her upper flesh decayed,
mutilated remains stuffed into a sack
clipped with her own bronze needle,
Still by this inner lip another woman
in a specially dug pit, an infant-size
niche cut into one corner of her
shallow circular dark. Her skull
sat apart from her crushed pelvis,
and her bones scattered like matchsticks.
In a corn-drying pit, another woman
with bad teeth, caries, abscesses
and arthritis, and that distortion
of the spine that comes from a lifetime
of heavy weights. Cut into the hillside
they uncovered a huge white face, almost
lost, with the moon's goggle eyes,
slingshots in the pupils, pebbles
in breast and rump: Ma-Gog, Mother
of the Staring Eyes who gave these hills
their name. Close by, in slightly later cuts,
the Horseman, his foreign cape flying,
horse all legs and fast lines,
eating up the land.

Home Movies

"Oh hear us when we cry to Thee
For those in peril on the sea"—
it seemed even then I knew
I was forcing the tears &
they were no less real for
being forced, since my father
was on the seas though the war
was no longer with us,
                              & before
assembly that morning, for
the first time, I'd tasted
oranges, or, to be exact,
a piece of orange skin
I'd lined up in
the playground to receive
from a kid whose father
must have saved him one
from the Yankee freighter
& we all ate the peel thinking
If this is an orange
you can have it

& running about the playground
not for fun but
because few had coats
& I registered in words
for the first time how
breath in the cold
grows wings,
& teachers, shivering like us,
kept us moving with threats
though some kids couldn't run
barefoot & those in clogs
preferred to clog-fight
like miners who
bet all their pay

& a day driving to Berwick
is honeysuckle
along lanes & the smell
of rabbits kept by the boy
whose parents we were visiting
who caught his finger in the cardoor
as we were leaving
& screamed & screamed &
the sickening screams
& smell of rabbits

& on mystery tour in
my uncle's bus
Aunt Violet grabbing my head
to bury but not before
I'd seen the blood
coursing down the gutter
like rainwater,
& later grabbing my head
again while in a loud voice
telling everybody to
"look at them doing it
in the field,"
& I knew what *it* was,
so she needn't have
buried my head.
I could smell her perfume
and trace the lace frill
round her petticoat and
watch shiny black shoes
with silver-buckle straps
& years later I dreamed
I killed her
& still haven't been caught

& my grandfather who
never went anywhere with us
& my grandmother who did
& told me my grandfather liked
his bit o'tail
which even then I found
a strange expression

& refusing to use
school toilets & arriving
every other day at
the backdoor
pants full
crying
& my grandmother hosing
me down on the
scullery floor
& on hot days
when the scent of hawthorn
made me think I had
lived somewhere else many times
she'd hold my wrists
under the ice-cold faucet & still
today I can see everything
in the house where I was born
as if I had never left it
& still picking wax flowers to roll
into balls in dark velvet-curtain rooms
huge with Christmas & the
ordinary wonder of the child's mind,
the pianola playing 'Custer's Last Stand,'
Uncle Arthur playing the organ
by ear under the gilt-framed
painting of shepherds
beside water and large rocks,
a scene I find myself still
trying to locate,
& the kettle's on the hob

for tea and hot-water bottles
& the bad-tempered tom's
in the oven
lying on fresh linen
while I watch the coal fire
send little messages upward
in soot-script
& my collie bitch is lying
across me on the sofa so
I can't move & can hardly
breathe—trained that way
my grandma says
to save lives in the snow

and all this I see
in a film running backwards
to my father in uniform
arriving at the house where
he'd been billeted.
My grandma shows him photos
of her daughter visiting
in London, builds her up.
And when my grandma
lets him think the house
is hers and not the colliery's,
and she is worth a bit, he's
already in love with my mother,
my blonde large-breasted mother.
And from her mother's letters
she's in love with him. So
home she hies &
marries in three weeks

The film runs down,
a flicker, stories
half-heard.
        The
lights go up
on an empty house.

(iv)
The Soul in Parenthesis

The Soul in Parenthesis

(A)

What

I sleep in the hayloft above horses.
   Bridles hang below like empty masks,
anatomies of the head; sinews without muscle,
   skin without bone. Blinkers cut off
eyes, huge black sockets.

   What are the names of the nights?
What are the nights called?

   And what is the name of the horse
in the story that had its head cut off
   but still continued to talk truth
because it loved a child so much?

Cold Gaps

From sandy breck the lark
    climbs her clear column of notes.
I throw stones to bring it down
    like a dust-devil, break
its force of continuity. But
    the stones pass clean through,
and coiled at the heather's roots
    and in its crisp stems
King Devil lies.

*

The yellowhammer's eggs
    with neat pinholes punched in
each end through which I blew
    her life's jelly
have cracked in my pocket.

    I am jolted by the cold gaps
between each slash of sun,
    and smell in the canalized stream
the dank sweat of old stormwater.
    My mother's underarm is elderblossom cool.

Sun-night

The chickens are vicious and uncanny.
   Their eyes flint chips.
Their necks when wrung go limp
   as little fingers.
You pull the tendons in their severed feet
   and the feet walk.
Chop off their heads
   and they run.

In their carcass, eggs move down
   toward birth, rubbery to hard.
Sometimes the white stone drops
   through the tacky hole
as they die.

   At night, Granda's torch is a yellow eye.
The ferrets' red eye has found
   the rats under the chicken house.

The foghorn lows. The fire
   is full of holes.
This night is called a made-up name.
   Granda calls it Sun-night.

(B)

Mirror

A child is alone in a large bed.
　His mother's voice is far away.
His eyes are trapped in the long mirror
　at the foot of the bed. It reflects him
onto the colorless wall. He cannot move.

　　　*

My mother takes out carved boxes
　with delicate drawers. Hands me
a ring, and tiny ivory elephants that are
　really hard white seeds. And coins and ribbons.
And a small black cat my father sewed
　into the lining of his uniform jacket
and kept there all through the war.
　And a bronze oak leaf for bravery.
And an official certified list
　of most of his wounds.

　　　*

On long Autumn evenings I stay
　in the valley with the cows.
One evening the earth under my feet
　shakes and turns red as the dry ox-blood
my grandmother uses on her tomato plants.
　And I know way down where I can't see,
coal seams are blue flames eating at
　the fathers of my friends. And I run
to the cows, lie down against their
　rumbling warm bellies, their bags
heavy on the dampening grass.

(C)

Orphans

Under stars, I hold a smoky quartz in my hand.
   At its heart, water trapped from an ancient sea
washes about, pure, cold, eternally distant.

   I look. Recall sassafras smoke natives made
and first white sailors smelled
   as they dropped the lead to a sandy bottom
in fourteen fathoms.
When the wind changed to northwest
the smoke was driven out to sea;
   dipped over earth's ball which Columbus said
rose like a woman's nipple at that place.

   I watch stars flake over the stream's hard face,
orphans alone in space.
   See childhood's last part: mother's two green
alabaster mermaids holding between them
   the bowl in which two fish gawp and dangle
in their tired element. They trail their shit
   behind them like banners or skywriting advertizing
"an empire of softness."

(D)

Time Up

In the living-room the radiator clanks
    like an old steamshovel.

My wife is playing a tape to talk
    cancer out of her body.
"Cancer cells are weak. It takes
    very little to flush them
out of the body. Picture this.
    Picture that. Picture your own body's
white blood cells. Picture.
    Picture."

                *

In the whorehouse across town,
    a tape is directing the whore's hand.
"Now my hand is moving to your head.
    You are. Very. Relaxed.
Very. Relax."

    If you open the eyes in your mask
just a slit you can see
    a bored whore obeying a machine.
The tape runs out.
    She tells you about the sore in her mouth.
That on Sundays she works a double shift.
    She tells you the hour is up.
Shadows of heads on the wall tell you
    the time is up. Time up.
She puts her other head back on her shoulders.
    You put your real head back on your shoulders.

(E)

Thunder in the Mirror

I dreamt my father dropped
  feetfirst into the lake.
He went in without a splash.
  No ripples, like an alligator
submerging. That night, someone rose
  from the dirt floor of my cabin.
He supported himself on his elbows
  as he talked to me, half in,
half out. Streaks of red barred his face
  and climbed the feathers in his hair.
Something you won't know about for years
  has happened in this house, he said.
That is all I came to tell you.
  Then he folded his arms and
sank without trace.
  He was wrong.
I knew.

  And now the sinking year is
  doubling its constellations.

  The lake stands still before Orion;
  turns over silent now.

  I am alone in a large bed.
  Thunder shakes in the mirror.

Following Through

Back up goes the cloud cover.
Flurries as far down as Hudson.
Power lines down.
Temperature down.
I am standing on an outcrop
watching a red kite across the valley
moving against the stream,
invisibly attached to the gray above
and the white below.

        In his cups my father spoke
           of incest as purest love
        and listed: a sister, brother-in-law,
           another sister, pleas for
        a daughter's love. . . .
           "Now that I've told you all this
        what do you think of me, more
           or less?"

        Mines
           grate along the hull
              midships
        under the wardroom & off
           between propellors.
        Torpedo track
        port,
              then
        the Number 1 Engine Room
           explodes
        with him in it.

        Everything happened in the Mays
        of different years. The E boat.
        The Luftwaffe. The sinking off Crete.
        His birthday. His deathday.

        On late night specials I have watched
        Noel Coward, with loyal ratings
        and noble officers, on his life-size
        model of the *Kelly*.

I will never know the real horror of those days
which are the parent horror of these.

A log has snapped.
Each end burns toward the other.
They meet in ash.
I am drying out.
My hair is still damp.
I throw on another scrawny piece
of chewed-up pine, torqued gray rope,
dead twist of the sun.
My ears start to hum.
I sense the cochlea's logarithmic spiral,
and the phyllotaxis of leaves,
one economy of movement that,
had he known it,
would have added one more pleasure
of order to his garden.

      The regimen is taped to one side
        of his desk:

   "1. Good physical and mental health.
    2. Good personal and intimate relations,

    such as those of marriage, the family,
    and friendships.

    3. The faculty for perceiving beauty
    in art and nature.

    4. A philosophy or religious point of view
    capable of coping successfully
    with the vicissitudes of life."

Two wild swans passed over,
   and the damnfool brother-in-law,
boasting to me of his clubs,
   honorary memberships, excited
by the 'famous' he'd taught to shoot,
   swung his twenty-year-old Jaguar
with his seventy-five-year-old arms
   round my father's hearse and headed
for the open road, not even the top
   of his head showing over
the wooden steering wheel.

A jarring in my bones
as I dig for the first time since creation
the swamp out back.
Silt had flowed like black blood
into the stream, and fanned out.

The land is bleeding to death.
Tonight, smoke heavy as mercury pushes up,
rises through the lamplight, lit gray.

A woman smell. Not in the small smoke,
but under, before it has burst its shell
and lies still beneath the damp bark.
Billows come back down the chimney,
running before night's quirt;
great gray canvas sails.
And I go out into the dark, naked,
my penis curved upward like a goat horn,
holding it in my hand,
a lead pipe, dark-veined flesh,
pointed stick.
Dawn grows green on it.
The morning star loosens in the sky
and glides about.
I am the flame that balloons from quiet
and consumes it all,
quiet and flame.

Enter the god of the oak-grove,
    he who will not go away,
swinging his dewlaps.

Echohawk had told me:
    "If you dream of fire, the only way
to prevent harm's to get up and start one
    right away. If you dream that buffaloes
or bulls are after you, it is bad.
    Dreams about yourself mean the opposite
of what they are. Follow them through."

The swishing of a tail that's a May storm.
    A gale from Gilgamesh. Fire and mud.
        Fire
glows at the center,
        settles
to be shaped, smooth as a peony
    for a child to pick up.
At the center of my palm is still
        the solar scar.

My hair feels like the hair of unborn calves.
                    His hair.

"If power doesn't want you, you'll never
    learn it. It is hard and there are many rules.
If you violate them, power gets after you."

The sudden panics of birds.
Plates of bluestone held by a horizontal band
of decayed rock.
A fern drops a cool tongue.
One touch, and the whole miniature mountainside
would tumble. We are traveling hundreds of miles a minute,
and it all stays up.

And in a dream a polevaulter
had risen toward the zenith, pushed away his support,
dropped, legs splayed like a breachbirth;
fallen on the other side of the hulk he leaped from.
The horizon wobbled like a whiplash,
rapped him across the hands.

There are black snakes in the roof.
Crossbeams tighten at a gust.
Night falls again, and all growth stops.
Gales rub the night sky till it glows.
Trees goats had gnawed
shed their silver bands.

> (A child is buried under the house.)
> (There are children buried under bridges.)

A father with ice and onions on his breath
lies in the crawlspace where yellowjackets holed out
all winter after I burned them out
of chinese-lantern nests.
The mice who stored birdseed
in beds and drawers
departed in the belly of some long-clawed Grendel
who sank his tracks in fine snow
from the corner of the house.

The seduction that fed
on fear and obedience. He kept on
tasting. Such queer
future. What was the name
of that "love" sucking
on me, a grown man, his
"fulfilled fantasy?"
And from him who had me plant
hedges of sharp thorn
and distrust warm dawns. . . .

Everywhere I turn,
everywhere I reach for the power
    of natural limits,
I find you there, old man.
    You who hated strangers
and have chosen me as your intimate.

    I am your stranger.
I will roll you up like one of the boundaries
    you crossed.

But everything is still very far from me.
What is at hand burns.
My face, your face, bursts out in sweat.
The chimney catches fire with a blast-furnace roar from hell.
I run out.
Sparks erupt,
drop heavy spirals onto shingles.
I grab the broken hose and spurt erratic loops upward
where I can't see.

            My hands are now reflections of the moon
            and seem far from me, two white birds,
            white as the fibrous eggs I saw under
            the pine-bark I tore off for the fire,
            and threw out of the door against the sky
        going over at a low angle,
    where the Bear was closer than life,
    closer than the small town
  under the ridge,
hidden in the furry glow of its lights.

Potlatch

My Fathers always said: Look to the Future,
and the present—they were always so busy
with the Future they never finished the sentence.

The Future. Naturally I agreed. Yes, *that*
would be worth it. Big winnings from big
sacrifices. So I brought out what few

coppers I had, and smashed them. A TV,
hi-fi, clothes, mirrors, bed, girls
(*not* books), everything, and set them

on fire, so the flames lit up my face
like the biggest copper of all. The
flare went far to putting out

my eyes. I thought I could see over oceans
and under clods. The heat twisted
my mouth. I thought it didn't

look so bad. Women would go for
that kind of thing. When I was
ready. For a while, at the back

of my eyes, like detached retinas,
skirts fluttered. Soon, smoke lit
from beneath began to roll in

like mist from a Saturday morning
horror movie. Then, as the Future
came closer, the flames burnt through,

redder, hotter, sometimes with the shape
of a squaw's vulva cut from her
and hanging from a cavalryman's

saddle, and darkness like the inside
of a peepshow settled in, till *at*
the Future I'd had enough. I called in

all my chips. Coppers, mirrors, hi-fi,
and all the rest, started to fall back
into themselves like objects in a film

run in reverse. I tried to make the thing
go forward. This, after all, was a
Comedy. I wanted my last act. But

objects fell from the screen right
on top of me, showering me with gifts. Bodies.
And glass. And limbs. My own body. My own limbs.

Two
The Middle of the Journey

Primal Scene

While they showered together,
to warm the house and give them
something to dress before,
I built a fire.
The smoke drove me out.
To clear the house I opened the window.
To warm the house I built up the fire.
To clear the smoke I opened the door.
Feathers flew away on the light,
and a splayed deer-track stood out
in the gleam of one star.
A moon with a piece taken out
sprayed phosphorescence over the snow's
long swathes pleated with
the blackest of trees,
till the wood gave up its damp
and flared for woman and child to
draw hearts by, and the child to trace
her name by, for the first time,
again and again.

Backlog

Smoke swayed from the chimney
  And drew across uncurtained windows.
All night the backlog lay low
  In buried fire.
In two beds they slept he and
  She at right angles.
At daybreak a fly prayed & backed into another fly.
  It treated the human arm as just
Another piece of wood.
  He rose,
Pulled his pyjama pants up to his armpits,
  Took out his penis & fitted
A black sock
  Over it.
Waking,
  She said:
Nothing is for ever.
  He lay two sticks across each other &
Across the log.
  He blew up a brief & then
A yellow flame.

All day the log sent smoke across the sun.

Spirits

Night falls like the old, real
night. Unconfined by screen doors,
shadows stretch and shrink.
A mosquito flies into the incandescent
mantle and drops in a plummet
of smoke. The childrens' flashlight flutters
from bedroom to living-room,
warding off sleep and its
monstered dark.
      I follow,
as in childhood I followed the
uncertain flight of fiery birds
on the hearth's soot
scratch the future's
wavering shape into the cold back
of a night rising from this
world of signs to
some other over
the unseen tops
of houses.

     Rain starts
to fall like the old, real
rain. Its lenses magnify
the dark. Tiny mirrors drop
behind reeds. A brief light strides
over the lake. An owl's pure breath
spits spirits.

The Truth

The birds come back in their cries
over bauchy snow. Six a.m. light
carries the little stream from
the quarry melt faster & faster
past the empty bird-feeder
that waits for the child to fill it
from a jar bigger than her pot belly.
But she is still asleep, wrapped
like a new-born near her mother,
snoring like a soldier, dreaming
perhaps of the icy stream she
washes her doll in, to get her
ready for the king of the mountains
and the people in the purple sky
she sings about who say
"you should be grateful for what
we've done for you."

I pad round the silent house,
the cold creeping into the
small of my back. I pick up
her drawings with their bug eyes,
crowns, and feet on sideways.
"Is it fair to expect the truth
from a child?" she'd asked.

The silence is so constant
it goes unnoticed. I hear as silence
one bird almost overhead calling
after the flock already in the pine-stand.

Everything is needed
less and less.

A Bird Passes

He puts out the light.
Glass of the skylight lets in the dark.
He sleeps while southeast rain
fills the quarry so it slips over logs
and leaves, sweeps away its surface
down the creek and past the locked door.
Soon it will block with maple leaves
and swamp the lawn cleared from goat-pasture
up to the door.
              He opens his eyes
and meets the rain sweeping across
a night only half begun. He remembers the spring
he dug out back.
              He sleeps again,
and his body takes the shape of his digging.
By the light trapped in rain he sees his arm
like a dead branch of white birch
outside the blanket.
              A bird, a blur
of a blacker black, flies over his head.
Water shaken from its wings
hits his cheek hard.

Ritual

My fire's smoke split
by the sun's trident
spread & settled into the world.
The sun's tin bird leaped
from inside the pond,
burning out my eye.

Now the moon's head floats
directly over my head
staring back up at it
through the skylight.
My head behind the moon
counts the lost hours,
so many broken teeth
dropped into night;
counts the shadows of fish
across the moon's face.

The moon flips, a little
jump as if its skin's
about to shed.
My hands go numb.
I hear the sounds of the cold,
the winds of space,
lifting the roof higher,
reaching for my face,
searching for its fire.

Indian Summer

Now the ducks are mostly gone, leaves
mostly fallen, antlers scraped clean
of velvet. The bears are fat and ready.

It is Indian summer, brief gold after
Squaw winter's cold rain. She sits on the balcony,
complaining of her head. I say

Look at the birds beside you: small pigeons.
She will not look. Someone crosses the pond
on a dinghy. She sees this: the small pond.

At the other side of the sea I notice
a yacht, and hear a cold yelp. She wakes.
An animal has been trapped, she says.

Ah, Wilderness!

The heat persisted though all the windows
  were thrown open
She trembled over snakes in the bed
  I ejected caterpillars from the sheets
The white birches refused to go dark
  and stood there all night
tall dumb ghosts

Next morning I turned round with my eyes shut
  many times
Took off in different directions
  Followed a deerpath that turned into a bridlepath
Thought I saw a snake
  Climbed a mountain
Found campers on the other side
  Tried to get lost
Stumbled on a road
  Walked deliberately in the wrong direction away from the
    cottage
Ended up in town
  Turned round again
Saw children taunting someone they called andrew
  Talked to andrew the idiot about barbed wire
Said he'd strung fence from here to albany
  What else do you want to know he asked
I closed my eyes
  Turn me around I asked
What he said
  The way home
I said

Fairy Tale

he fed the horse in its soft mouth.
it dunged and he turned into the palace,
its glass veranda and plants. he'd
married the princess and now went
looking for her. he knew the queen mother
disapproved though she was nowhere
to be seen. a footman approached
with a silver tray and nothing on it.
the footman pointed to the flowered carpet
under his feet and left.
the man put his toe under the carpet
and found another underneath. he got
the message and left for ever.
outside the horse too had gone.
and its soft mouth.

Legend

There's no way back, he called as she stood
on the loose shale at the top
of the quarry face and cried out.

The water was lower than summer. Insects spun
after night's rain. Frogs screamed & became
bubbles. He kicked the crickets from his feet,

Treked across swamp ground. Crows
shifted their wings sideways in flight,
predicting winter. Earth began losing light.

> "I considered myself an owl
> but the owls are hooting
> and now
> I fear the night."

Leaving

Just before it thinks it's
going to die, it blooms. Runs up

a flower spike. One splash
of water after a drought makes

up its mind. Hence water signifies
death. And the house signifies

absurdity: light silver windows,
someone standing in the open door.

The idea's not to leave. But
the stairs lead down. He is about

to take them when fire breaks out
and leaps across the valley.

The phones are all on hold. A
war is on. The voice on hold says

keep holding. It begins to rain.
Lights are a sea-snake wandering off.

And the moon on the broken water
is a slick stalk, dumb, scented, redundant.

Unknowing

On the faucet's lip
the drop
gathers to a sun
and explodes
shatters the whole window
augments breaking day

The rasp of his blood is still in her ears
Sharp crumbs scratch her breath
Words thin on her lips
to say
she must know
if the glass shivered to a ghost
before her hand
crossed his face
before her face stood in his

For now
he is
one wing
split image of an invisible second
that may never have been
She follows
hoping to know
to find him if not whole then
flown together
fused in divorce
that will leave her able
to thrust against live air

But her own shadow darkens
her sight
Her eyes shatter and get underfoot
and she dreams that
the ghost enters his unmarred glass
and lies down quietly
As light crosses his face
he seems alive
a chill in crystal

She will never really know
when he died or if
or by whose hand
but now she knows
she must fly in the migrant season
where waves break
where each drop lies broken in a whole reflective body
whose mica skin shivers
at each sunburst
and buckles again in cloud
to fine invisibility

The Middle of the Journey

Nel mezzo del cammin di nostra vita
mi ritrovai per un selva oscura,
che la diritta via era smarrita . . .
                    (*Inferno*, Canto 1)

1

I lie in bed. Under my eyes, two
lines of snow like the canals

On Mars run down to a horizontal
lake mid-mountain. A town

Is seen over roofs of turning wheat,
blue-green. Red roofs, scarlet poppies,

In ditches. Valerian patches. More
red roofs like further fallen poppies,

Thrust and counter-thrust; parry
and surrender. It is not somewhere

I have been. Perhaps it is
somewhere I am going.

2

The valley's long sound is
heightened by the silence. Hanging

In the silk-sound of the stream,
chickadees count invisible events

On the undersides of leaves. I
turn, and look back as if I could

Count each step that comes
straight at me, the grass lifting

Back up, paler. I stand where
the sky's axe-edge notches

The hill's top. If I could look at
my life now, it would be like finding

An old scratched daguerreotype of
someone I recognized but could not name.

3

Daybreak. The comfortless wind
resists the comfort of sunrise.

Moths come too late, when the earth
has just turned. I mistake the moths

For snow, and the wind that clips
the curtain I mistake for

The wind that brings
bees and the metal scent

Of old lilacs. Fissures
in rock expand their darkness.

4

Under my window a boy whistles
a tune so offkey and crude he must

Have made it up himself. The mind's
corners open. Snow begins to fall

Like the last light squeezed from leaves.
I lie in the dark, letting the season's

Final mosquito do with me what she wills.
I am floating just above my body,

My body dark, dreaming me, the
future, making itself up, linking

Itself to my discontinuity,
covering me like the embroidered

Bedspread my grandmother made
long before I was born.

40

Dawn, crisscross, falters
in shadows of shadows which were
themselves like frightened breathing.

Too soon, distance is here,
sturdy as a rose's long stem,
tapping at the glass.

Zero at the Bone

block of ice.
flowers inside.
flowers on the outside.
ten draught-horses inside, pulling.
ten draught-horses on the outside, pulling.
                              stalemate.
flowers in the grass, pulling.
                    stalemate.
ice in the sky, pulling.
                stalemate.
the whole north pole,
the whole south pole, pulling.
                         stalemate.
one flower growing out of the ice.
one flower growing into the ice.
                         stalemate.

the axis tips.
the poles change.
the horses are freed.
the flowers rot.
new ones spring up.
the earth swings off course a few degrees.
zones change.
people move.
the light is the same, give or take a few minutes either way.
the dead in the change move off.
the living attain more memories.
                         stalemate.

Driving Off

In deserted piazzas cars park
   like tombstones. A stain appears
on an upstairs window, and
   disappears. The new nightwatchman
emerges: "You want something,
   you?" How can 'you' explain? Do
you reveal who you are on a piazza
   where the light of day was a
small construction without style that
   used prescribed materials, and
night's light is an old swaying lamp
   that hides more than it reaches?
The piazza, you could say to him, is
   a souvenir, a concrete expression,
of which one should take note. You
   could say that. Or you could think
in the dark: The years have passed here,
   discrete as a famous man of culture
about to take his own life, son of a
   priest, raised in the town with all
its once rich folklore which he had
   drawn upon. A man who had set
the last chapter of his last novel
   in a deserted piazza with cars
parked like tombstones, from where,
   on a clear day, one can still see the
thin tracks between mountain crests and
   the only surviving church that serves
as chapel, necropolis, official program,
   Party office, all in one: parabola of
the prodigious. Yes, you could think to
   yourself, he achieved successful
illusions. But perhaps you will go on to
   ask yourself if its representation
to the nightwatchman wouldn't dangerously
   signify the re-forming of an allegiance.

So, silently, surrounded by black cobbles,
and the sudden apparition of a new
ideal with its own (caricatured?) images,
you open the door of one of the cars,
pretending it is yours, climb in, and make
as if to drive off.

Like Boats

Who is this has come in
    and changed all the bedclothes,
folded them into neat piles in the closet
    so I don't know what
belongs where?

                Who
sent the cutlery into oblivion
    so I've had to eat everything
with my fingers?

                And who
sprayed milkweed with
    Krylon Acrylic Spray
and left the can with a wreath
    of dead daisies?

The rain knows no bounds.
    It has smothered horizons.
Mist sneaks into the house,
    and I burn the cheap bonded-sawdust
shed roof that collapsed
    in the first storm.

I collapse onto the sofa.
    Where are the insects?
The yellowjacket who stung me
    as I sat on the toilet
last time up; who almost
    killed me as I felt my heart
stop, then kick up again
    as I drove, dead, twenty miles
to the nearest clinic
    for allergy tests that
have set me back months?
    And where are my spiders
who eat my flies? And where
    are my flies?

She's
exploded a bomb! I know
    its results. I'd done the same
two summers back, when the
    bank president's hippy
vegetarian daughter, who couldn't
    kill a living thing, had filled
the house with birds, who'd
    filled the house with fleas.
Who'd never paid her rent.

I toss the orderly weeds
    into the back of the damp fire.
And dusty caterpillars of goldenrod
    she'd perched in a precarious
glass vase over the fireplace
    drop, and shatter.

Where are the flies?
    Above the dash of the rain
I hear a small buzz.
    One dazed black fly
greets me like an old hound
    from the corner of a chair.

In the night
    rain ate into my sleep.
I woke in my sleep
    and it stopped.
I woke,
    and rain
had obliterated all distinction.

The glare of separation was in the room.

I push everything away from my life
    like boats.

Joy

Dawn arrived: a cat
with a bird in its mouth,
stepping dark and deliberate
toward my bed. But a bird
I'd never heard anywhere before,
let alone in this city,
banged his little drum
down by the fountains
which had not yet started up
under my window.
In my head an Armenian nightingale
rose again like
smoke through water.

That day, all day, I hummed
a Hindi love song from some
Indian movie, all round town,
through the scent of the park's
new-cut grass and mayflower
in all its almost-sinister
sweetness of my childhood.
A squirrel came down his manicured tree
whiskers first, snuffled
through whatever feathery seeds
were left on the grass, and
threw himself into the air,
a whiplash, hooked salmon,
glove turned inside out.